Life is like a game of croquet. The stake is the goal but the next wicket is most important.

To: _____
From: _____
Occasion: _____
Date: _____

© Tad Pritchett 2016
Published by Molly Luvblossum Press
Editor: Dee Driver-Pritchett
Illustrator: Bobbi Showalter

The Road From Teenager To Adult Can Be Rough But Here Are Some Obvious Tips

THE TENUOUS ART OF BECOMING A SUCCESSFUL ADULT

LESSONS FROM THE BUTTERFLY

Every living creature, animal or plant, makes the journey from seed to tree, baby to adult.

Even the Earth, inanimate yet dynamic, changes as it ages. Elements evolve, the universe shifts and everything must re-style to successfully survive.

The road to adulthood insinuates a specific path from birth to successful flight but what is seldom revealed to us is the hidden journey.

The caterpillar makes its journey seemingly in the open. The human journey seems more mysterious. But the successful butterfly teaches us lessons.

LESSONS FROM THE BUTTERFLY

We have the same path to travel and we have lessons that guide us to being a successful adult. The big difference is that we are gifted with an internal GPS that pushes us to investigate our surroundings, to learn and to discover.

That gift has brought us from the valley of origin to a human on every block. Our curiosity has shepherded us from rock tools to spacecraft.

With all the good has also come misguided curiosity, crumbling the path to being a successful adult.

As with the caterpillar, we have lessons. When she practices them she becomes a butterfly. When we control our curiosity we stay on the path to becoming adults.

Dear Caterpillar, you have been appointed by Mother Nature to be inducted into adulthood. As an adult candidate, there are some behavioral by-laws that you need to consider. I hear you want to move away on your own, learn some life skills and grow up. I have heard that your project completion date to become an adult is within four years.

So, in the next four years you want to transform yourself from a cool high school caterpillar to an independent adult butterfly who can fly on their own. WOW! That is an incredibly difficult transformation that only Mother Nature seems to flawlessly handle and she has rules of engagement that you need to know.

And you, a mere teenager, yearns to do the same thing, transforming into a young adult. You will make your own way and live by the decisions that you alone will make.

Well, I have been an adult for a while and I will tell you it is a very difficult assignment that in retrospect I really underestimated. Actually, the reality is we all do. So I thought it might be the time to tell you about the birds and bees that an adult butterfly will learn.

Every adult has made the transition from caterpillar. Some ended up as butterflies and some ended up simply as flies.

The flies most likely failed at least one of these lessons, lessons that they could have learned from others if they had only asked. Their curiosity took over good sense.

When we are caterpillars we only know what we crawl over and eat. We don't yet know of the wonders of life that flying will bring to us. The wonders will come when we learn from others, learn from those who have experienced the flight. But we have to observe and we have to ask.

There are over seven billion humans inhabiting this planet and it is estimated that there have been over 100 billion humans since humans arrived on the scene. That is a lot of experience and it is hard to believe that any problem we have has not been faced by one of the 100 billion experiences. Just remember, everyone has a story so stop, listen and learn.

So I have some suggestions that I have found to be very important in making the transition from caterpillar to butterfly. They are a simple list of the obvious but their execution can be problematic.

I call them The Lessons From the Butterfly

1st BUTTERFLY LESSON
I AM RESPONSIBLE FOR MYSELF!

2nd BUTTERFLY LESSON
FAILURE DOESN'T JUST HAPPEN!

3rd BUTTERFLY LESSON
DO WHAT THE SITUATION REQUIRES!

CHAPTER I

I AM RESPONSIBLE FOR MYSELF

The Keystone of a Successful Life

Domains

How many times have we felt relieved that we can blame something else for our mistakes? Kids are very innovative when they squirm out of being responsible for their own behavior. Mom did it, Dad did it, the teacher didn't like me or my alarm clock didn't go off. So what? You are still the one who lost out somehow either missing an important event or performing poorly.

By not taking responsibility for yourself you are letting others control your life and how you live your life. Life is competitive, competing for what you have and who you are. If you let others take responsibility for your behavior they will determine who you are.

You will make decisions and live with the consequences. Think about it.

Before, your domain was defined by your parents. They decided who you could play with, where you would go, and what you could watch on TV. They told you when to go to bed and got you to your appointments on time. They created your domain and approved of any changes you might think necessary. Their responsibility was to avoid train wrecks that the wrong domain might harbor.

When something derailed you could run home or call Mom but all of a sudden you are now an adult. Why didn't someone tell me this might happen? Nobody will tell you, "Hey, get up and go to class."

You alone will be responsible for that and all other decisions in your domain that will determine your life. You have a new domain of acquaintances, friends, and experiences. Take responsibility for what is in your domain and be very protective of who and what is allowed inside.

Select responsible friends who ask how you are, or how they can help before telling you about themselves. Your domain should inspire confidence not self-doubt and infuse your life with peace, not provoke strife.

Your domain is a mosaic of the people and surroundings that meld your life. You will develop effective ways of holding them accountable, not make excuses for them. Create a domain that will make you successful and will keep you at peace with yourself.

Responsibility for your failures and successes must be integrated into every aspect of your life. Blaming others is a quick road to failure.

There are three attributes about people that are hard wired and change-resistant. They are intelligence, character, and the willingness to work hard. Intelligent domain members will challenge you to think ahead to avoid failure. People with character will teach you reponsibility and hard workers will teach you that your best is not good enough and push you to do what the situation requires. These are all aspects of being a successful adult.

Knowledge and Courage

To be responsible you must develop both knowledge and courage. First is having the knowledge to make decisions for yourself. You are heading toward a plethora of knowledge, the horn of plenty for experiences and your success will be determined by how well you take responsibility for yourself. Secondly, you will be responsible for absorbing that knowledge but you will need the courage to do what is right and stand up for yourself!

You have a great basis for knowing the right thing but sometimes the wrong thing seems right. This is when you need the courage to look into your life and ask yourself, "Will my family be proud of me if I do this?" Or maybe a more important question is, "Will I be proud of myself and my behavior?"

Everyone comes to crossroads in their lives, when they look back up the path and reevaluate their behavior, everyone. So the question, "will I be proud of myself" will always be the most important litmus test of your behavior. Do not let a shoddy and haphazardly assembled domain lead your life, you now must lead your domain.

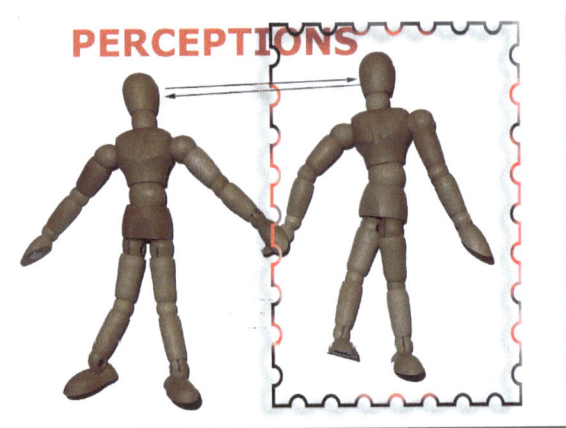

Perceptions

Many times the hard path is the right path. Nothing comes easy so if a choice is the path that looks too good to be true, it probably is.

"To thine own self be true." This was a father's advice in Shakespeare's Hamlet. We exist through other's perceptions of us so manage those perceptions, but be true to yourself.

Other people's perceptions of us form the basis of who we really are. We may look at ourselves with loath while others see us with love and admiration. Embrace that perception. Seek out others perceptions in your domain and grow from what you learn but determine your own self-worth.

Be in tune with what others in your domain think of you and learn who you really are. It makes no difference that we hold ourselves in high regard if others think we are jerks. It is much easier to perpetuate a good first impression than do damage control on a poor one.

Our legacy is in what others remember of us and nobody is a given in your domain. They are there because you and THEY want to be there. Respect them.

Life's Mechanics

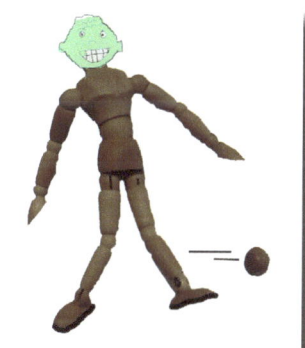

I have always found that exceptional adults develop routines that make the maintenance of life automatic through repetition. Practice routines until you learn the right way to do things and then practice more until there is no chance that you will fail. This is especially true in mastering "life's mechanics." In everyone's life there are routine tasks that have to be tended to just to keep our heads above water. They continue to run in the background of our lives.

When left to their own devises your life becomes disorganized. You become a life firefighter, all the time putting out fires in your life.

Here is an example of a list of Life Mechanics that you must master:

1. Get up on time and make your bed.
2. Maintain personal hygiene regularly.
3. Clean your bathroom, do your laundry.
4. Pick up after yourself, fix your own meals.
5. Know and obey laws, use public transportation.
6. Study and keep up with your work.
7. Have sufficient school supplies.
8. Know your professors and their office locations.
9. Maintain your checkbook and credit cards.
10. Communicate with your parents and others.

As you assess your new domain, list the tasks that must be successfully performed to keep your life running. These things include the basics of living like eating, budgeting your money, washing your clothes and taking care of yourself.

One of the most important and ignored basic skills you should practice is effective communication. Anticipate situations and practice what might be your response. Learn to defend yourself in a constructive fashion so that others know you are strong but understanding.

Remember, communication is exchanging, not just delivering information. An important and often overlooked aspect of learning is listening for content, not just response. Not only will you learn but you will reinforce the importance of those in your domain.

Communication is a survival skill that will connect you to your domain. It represents you and is an essential conduit to your domain.

Life's mechanics will form the foundation of your success in taking responsibility for every aspect of your life. The successful management of life's mechanics will determine your happiness and security.

1st BUTTERFLY LESSON

I AM RESPONSIBLE FOR MYSELF!

BUTTERFLY LESSONS CHECKLIST
AM I RESPONSIBLE?
Weekly Guide

Rate your behavior on a scale of 1-10. 10 is best, 1 requires work

1. Did I blame others
2. Did I like my domain
3. Did I make knowledgeable decisions
4. Am I managing perceptions
5. Am I taking care of life mechanics
6. Am I practicing routines
7. Am I practicing effective communication
8. Did I listen for content

   Total score This week _____

   Score Last Week   _____

   Improvement: _____

   Example of any of the above:

CHAPTER II

FAILURE DOESN'T HAPPEN ALL AT ONCE

Stealthy Fruition

Learn from others. You will find that there really isn't much new; it is only history that we have not learned.

In other words, many in history have experienced the same steps to failure. A successful adult seeks out those experiences others have had to learn and to utilize them in their own pursuit of success.

You will learn about failure and you will learn that failure doesn't define you but how you handled it will. Everyone who tries fails but a successful adult learns how to build upon failure and become better.

Seldom are we presented with an intervention as powerful as failure that offers the opportunities for real improvement. The process or actions that we are following slows or stops. It gives us a breather to step back and ask ourselves how can I take advantage of this break to recover and upgrade my product.

But I learned that failure doesn't just happen, it comes to fruition in small stealthy steps. It was up to me to learn how to see those small, sometimes invisible steps in advance and change course to head off failure.

In a good movie the music sounds the alarm that failure of some variety is imminent but in the real world there is never an orchestra to blare out danger.

We must learn to think things through, look for roadblocks and traps.

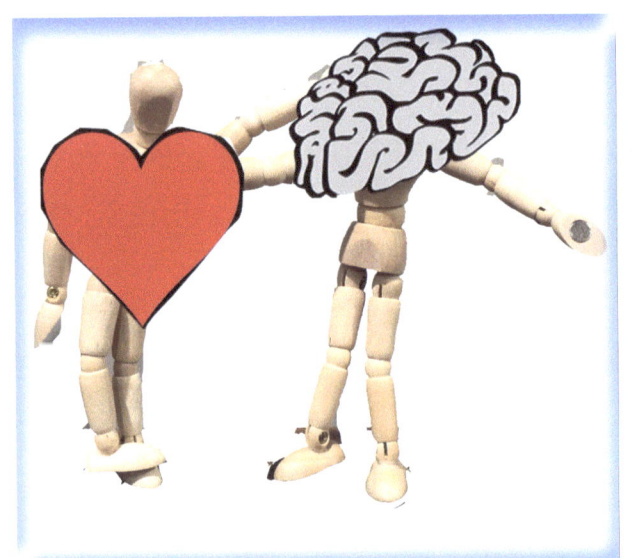

There are always signs that things are going badly but we cannot see them. If you have built a supportive domain, it will tell you.

When we are younger we tend to make decisions from the heart, not the mind. The mind is not yet programed with the necessary experience to overrule the heart. As you gain experience in life, over time your heart and mind will become one.

But the heart fails to see the little steps that lead to failure and it has a powerful voice. Listen to your mind; think about the possibility that the steps directed by the heart are really the tiny steps toward failure. We have all been there.

Your mind might recommend a consultation with someone with relevant experiences. But our ego teams up with the heart and we trudge ahead, a valuable learning opportunity is lost.

You need to understand that you exist as four entities. First there is the person we know within ourselves but do not want our domain to see or know. Usually our inner self is constantly looking for validation and paths to success. Do not be oblivious to the valuable perspective of others.

Then there is the individual that we and our domain know. Some call it our "sales sample," others call it our "good side." Regardless of what we call it, that part of us is sometimes blind to the silent steps to failure because we are trying to impress our domain. We can become so busy inflating our sales sample we think we can propel our Titanic through the icebergs on our own.

Thirdly, there is a view of us that our domain knows, but we don't see ourselves. These are valuable perceptions assembled in bits and pieces. They are nuggets of truth that we need to tap, in our quest for being an adult and avoiding the little steps to failure. A healthy domain will help us see our blind spots.

Finally, there is a part of us that is unknown to us and our domain. It is our undiscovered potential, our innate ability to explore and learn. A supportive domain will provide a safe environment for discovering your potential by avoiding the hidden steps to failure.

Seek harmony between your heart, your mind and your domain. As you evaluate situations and determine courses of action, always have the courage to check to make sure they are all equal players who have equal say in determining those small, imperceptible steps that lead to success or failure.

Heart • Mind • Domain

2nd BUTTERFLY LESSON

FAILURE DOESN'T JUST HAPPEN!

BUTTERFLY CHECKLISTS
Failure Doesn't Just Happen
Weekly Guide

Rate your behavior on a scale of 1-10. 10 is best, 1 requires work

1. Did I have any failures this week
2. Did I anticipate and head off any failures
3. Did I let my domain make decisions for me
4. Are my heart, mind and domain one
5. Did I stand up for myself
6. Did I alter plans when needed
7. Did I use a failure as an opportunity to improve

   Total score This week _____

   Total Score Last Week _____

   Improvement: _____

   Example of a failure and an Example of avoiding one:

CHAPTER III

DO WHAT THE SITUATION REQUIRES

Your Best of the Past Is Not Good Enough

Maybe the hardest lesson to learn in the quest to be an adult is simply that our best efforts of the past are not good enough for being an adult. You must do what the situation requires. When you do what the situation demands, you grow and do things you never thought possible.

Successful adults don't limit their horizons by "doing their best," an excuse shared by all mediocre adults. It is great to do your best all the time but to grow you must risk failure. Tap into the unknown part of yourself and stretch your achievements. Ask your domain for help.

Fear of failure stunts growth. The truly successful adults do what the situation requires. You don't learn Calculus, Physics or to play the violin by doing your best, you do what is required.

The hard way is usually the right way. Take risks and set goals that require you to stretch and extend your talents. When you take risks that challenge you beyond anything else you have ever accomplished you grow in confidence.

If it looks like a course of action will not accomplish your goals, do not lower your goals. Change what you are doing even if it requires you to learn something new. You grow by taking risks and doing what the situation demands and many times the situation demands new plans.

Nothing demotivates more than inaction and nothing energizes more than accomplishing goals. As you develop action steps to accomplish goals you will also discover paths to avoid failure.

Growth will bring success to your life. You will become more and more essential, more effective, more powerful.

Your heart will tell you when to be responsible for yourself. It will know. Your mind will think through the small, sometimes hidden and imperceptible steps to failure and will alert you. Your domain will disclose to you what is required!

Finally...

Finally, when the sun begins to drop in the west and the butterfly is at rest, her wings furled for the night, she will look at the reflection cast into her heart. Do I like this creation and do I know who she I really is? She will be peering at her creator because she was responsible for her own creation.

Heart • Mind • Domain
All One

IT'S AN EXCITING FLIGHT!

You Will Do Great!

3rd BUTTERFLY LESSON
DO WHAT THE SITUATION REQUIRES!

BUTTERFLY CHECKLISTS
Do What the Situation Requires

Rate your behavior on a scale of 1-10. 10 is best, 1 requires work

1. When did I take action when needed

2. When did I do what the situation requires and it was better than my best

3. Did I adjust my goals or did I learn something new

4. Did my domain motivate me to accomplish something I had never done before

Total score This week ____

Score Last Week ____

Improvement: ____

Example of any of the above:

In Summary
Pick Your Domain Wisely

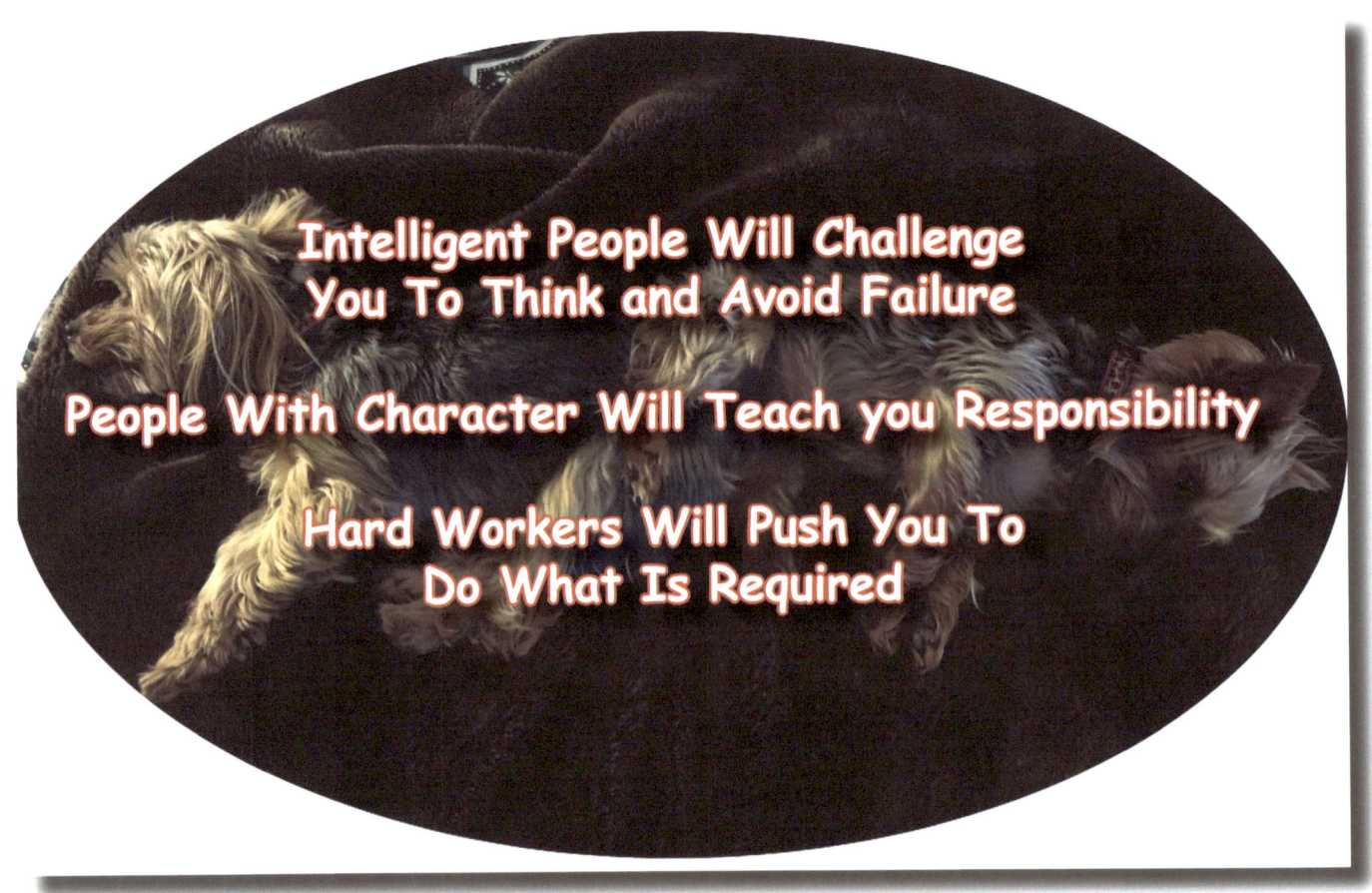

Intelligent People Will Challenge You To Think and Avoid Failure

People With Character Will Teach you Responsibility

Hard Workers Will Push You To Do What Is Required

Be An Adult

I AM RESPONSIBLE FOR MYSELF

FAILURE DOESN'T JUST HAPPEN

DO WHAT THE SITUATION REQUIRES

Be An Adult
Preserve Their Habitat